The Let's Talk Library

Let's Talk About Alcohol Abuse

Marianne Johnston

The Rosen Publishing Group's

PowerKids Press

New York

Published in 1996 by The Rosen Publishing Group, Inc.
29 East 21st Street, New York, NY 10010

First Edition

Photo credits: Cover by Guillermina DeFerrari; p. 4 by Michael Brandt; p. 20 by Lauren Piperno; all other photos by Guillermina DeFerrari.

Book Design and Layout: Erin McKenna

Johnston, Marianne.
    Let's talk about alcohol abuse / Marianne Johnston.
       p.   cm. — (The let's talk library)
    Includes index.
    Summary: Explains what alcohol is, who may drink it, how it affects the brain and body as well as the personality, how to deal with peer pressure to drink and related matters.
    ISBN 0-8239-2303-7
    1. Alcoholism—Juvenile literature. 2. Drinking of alcoholic beverages—Juvenile literature.[1. Alcohol.] I. Title. II. Series.
HV 5066.J63   1996
362.29'2—dc20   95-26714
                                   CIP
                                   AC

Manufactured in the United States of America

Table of Contents

What Is Alcohol?

Alcohol is a drug that is in some drinks. Beer and wine are the most common. You may have seen these drinks at the grocery store or in your own refrigerator at home.

Even though some people drink alcohol, it can be dangerous and can cause many problems.

◀ You may have seen drinks that have alcohol in them in your own house.

Alcohol Is Just for Grown-ups

Even though alcohol is a drug, it is not against the law for people to drink it once they are 21 or older. If you are not 21 yet, you cannot drink alcohol without breaking the law. When you turn 21, you can decide whether you want to drink alcohol or not. But if you are smart you will learn to drink alcohol **responsibly** (re-SPON-si-blee), so that it doesn't hurt you or others.

Signs like this one say that a person must be over 21 years old to drink alcohol. ▶

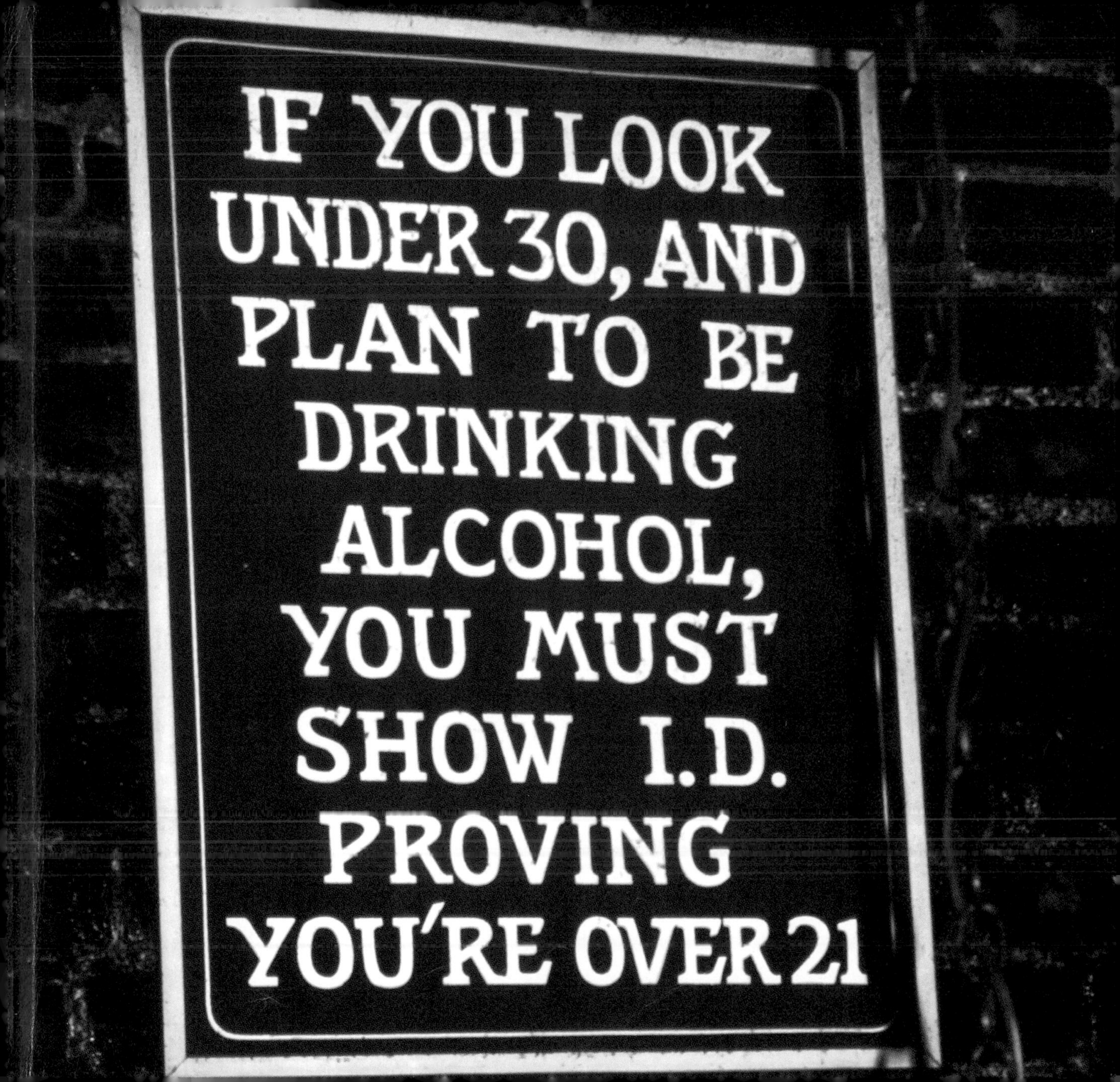
IF YOU LOOK
UNDER 30, AND
PLAN TO BE
DRINKING
ALCOHOL,
YOU MUST
SHOW I.D.
PROVING
YOU'RE OVER 21

If Your Parents Drink

Have you ever seen your parents have a beer or drink a glass of wine? It is **legal** (LEE-gul) for them to do this because they are at least 21 years old. Many adults drink alcohol at parties or at mealtimes.

But just because your parents might drink alcohol sometimes doesn't mean that you will choose to when you are older.

◀ It is legal for adults to drink alcohol.

Alcohol and Your Brain

Did you know that your brain controls everything your body does? It allows you to walk, talk, breathe, and think. But when alcohol is in a person's body, his brain slows down and doesn't work as well as it could.

If the brain isn't working right, the body can't work right either. This can make a person behave differently.

Even a little alcohol with dinner can affect how a person thinks and acts. ▶

Alcohol Affects Your Body

When a person drinks alcohol, he has a harder time doing normal things. The more alcohol someone drinks, the harder it is for him to speak or to drive a car. Sometimes people drink so much that they even have a hard time walking. Alcohol also makes it hard to think clearly. Someone who is drinking alcohol might say things that don't make sense or might take risks he wouldn't usually take.

◀ A person who has drunk too much alcohol may have a hard time walking.

Alcohol Can Make You Sick

Drinking too much alcohol can make a person sick. This is called alcohol abuse. And if a person drinks too much, it can make her so sick that she throws up.

Some people drink too much alcohol for many years. This is very bad for a person's **health** (HELTH). When a person drinks alcohol, his body can't work right. It becomes tired and sick more often.

Drinking too much alcohol can make a person sick to her stomach. ▶

Alcoholism

People can become **addicted** (a-DIK-ted) to alcohol. This means that they think they need to drink alcohol to deal with everyday life. People who are addicted to alcohol are called **alcoholics** (al-coe-HAW-liks).

Being addicted can make someone do poorly at work or forget important days like birthdays. An alcoholic loses control of a lot of things in his life. He may make his family very sad.

◀ An alcoholic thinks he needs alcohol more than anything else in his life.

17

How Does Alcohol Affect People?

Alcohol can affect people differently. Sometimes their **personalities** (pur-sun-AL-i-tees) change. Some people seem happier and laugh a lot. Some people become angry when they drink alcohol. Some people become sad when they drink alcohol.

There is no way to know how someone will act when alcohol is in his body. That is one of the reasons why it is so dangerous.

You never know how someone will react when he drinks alcohol. ▶

Alcohol Abuse Affects Everyone

When a person drinks too much, it is said that he is drunk. Alcoholics are often drunk. Someone who is drunk may do things he wouldn't normally do. He may get really angry. He may yell or hit someone. He may try to drive even though his body isn't prepared to do so. Lots of accidents are caused by people who try to drive when they are drunk. You see, being drunk affects the person drinking and everyone around him.

◀ Every family member feels the
affects of alcohol abuse.

Peer Pressure

Some of your friends may try alcohol to see what it is like. They might want you to try it with them. When friends try to force you to do something you don't want to do, it is called **peer pressure** (PEER PRE-shur).

If this happens, the best thing to do is to be strong and say no. A real friend will stay your friend even if you don't drink alcohol.

Glossary

addicted (a-DIK-ted) When someone needs a drug to deal with everyday life.

alcoholic (al-coe-HAW-lik) Someone who is addicted to alcohol.

health (HELTH) How well or sick your body is.

legal (LEE-gul) Allowed by the law.

peer pressure (PEER PRE-shur) When people your age try to make you do something you don't want to.

personality (pur-sun-AL-i-tee) Set of qualities you have that make you you.

responsible (re-SPON-si-bul) Doing something in a way that won't hurt you or someone else.

Index